GW00715585

The Intruders

A Comedy

Peter Horsler

Samuel French—London
New York – Sydney – Toronto – Hollywood

© 1981 BY SAMUEL FRENCH LTD

This play is fully protected under the Copyright Laws of the British Commonwealth of Nations, the United States of America and all countries of the Berne and Universal Copyright Conventions.

All rights, including Stage, Motion Picture, Radio, Television, Public Reading, and Translation into Foreign Languages, are strictly reserved.

No part of this publication may lawfully be transmitted, stored in a retrieval system, or reproduced in any form or by any means, electronic, mechanical, photocopying, manuscript, typescript, recording, or otherwise, without the prior permission of the copyright owners.

Rights of Performance by Amateurs are controlled by SAMUEL FRENCH LTD, 26 SOUTHAMPTON STREET, LONDON WC2E 7JE, and they, or their authorized agents, issue licences to amateurs on payment of a fee. **It is an infringement of the Copyright to give any performance or public reading of the play before the fee has been paid and the licence issued.**

Licences are issued subject to the understanding that it shall be made clear in all advertising matter that the audience will witness an amateur performance; that the names of the authors of the plays shall be included on all announcements and on all programmes; and that the integrity of the author's work will be preserved.

The Royalty Fee indicated below is subject to contract and subject to variation at the sole discretion of Samuel French Ltd.

Basic fee for each and every
performance by amateurs   Code D
in the British Isles

In Theatres or Halls seating Six Hundred or more the fee will be subject to negotiation.

In Territories Overseas the fee quoted above may not apply. A fee will be quoted on application to our local authorized agent, or if there is no such agent, on application to Samuel French Ltd, London.

ISBN 0 573 12115 X

ESSEX COUNTY LIBRARY

Please note our NEW ADDRESS:

Samuel French Ltd
52 Fitzroy Street London W1P 6JR
Tel: 01 - 387 9373

822.914

EY37706

CHARACTERS

Bill Smith
Adrian Smythe
Helen Smythe
Linda

The action takes place in the lounge of a detached, sub-urban house

Time—the present

THE INTRUDERS

The lounge of a detached, suburban house. The early hours of the morning

There are french windows UC with heavy curtains drawn back to show that it is night. The only door to the room is UR and obviously leads to the rest of the house. UL there is a small bureau with a telephone set on it and a chair in front of it. RC there is a settee with a small coffee table set below it, an armchair DL and a small bookcase DR. There are a number of small, valuable ornaments on the bookcase and bureau

When the CURTAIN rises, the stage is empty, lit only by faint moonlight filtering through the french windows. Immediately the burglar, Bill Smith, and his accomplice, Linda, appear in silhouette outside the windows, making it very obvious that she is in the late stages of pregnancy. Bill shines a shielded torch on the lock of the door while Linda looks from left to right, showing that her task is to keep watch. He succeeds in opening the french windows and waves her away to hide somewhere outside

Linda disappears from view

Bill steps warily into the room, then, sizing up the place by shining the torch around, he moves down to the bookcase and examines the ornaments on it. Undoing his jacket, he reveals a small bag attached to the lining into which he places the ornaments one by one before crossing to the bureau to repeat the operation. Then, feeling in his jacket pocket, he produces a small instrument and begins to tackle the bureau lock

The hall door opens silently and Adrian Smythe appears, dressed in a dressing-gown and carrying a poker. He stands in the doorway for a moment watching Bill and then suddenly flicks on the lights

Bill (*turning sharply*) A-ah!
Adrian (*with raised poker*) Quite still now, quite still or I'll fell

you with one blow! (*He moves warily to the windows with his eyes fixed firmly on Bill*) I think we'll close these. (*He draws the curtains*) Posted a look-out, have we? Don't want to alarm them. (*Indicating to Bill to move* RC) Now, move away from that desk!

Bill backs to RC

That's far enough! Don't get any ideas of dashing for the door. I'll crack your skull if I have to.

Bill All right, all right, no need for that, guv, I'm beat. Won't give yer no trouble. Ain't a violent man, I ain't.

Adrian Well, I can be, so you stay very still while I phone for the police. (*Without taking his eyes off Bill, he moves to the telephone and picks up the receiver*) If you as much as move a muscle—

Bill Please, guv, don't do it! I know I ain't got no right—I'll get ten years this time—please, guv. Hit me with that poker. Rather be done in, honest I would.

Adrian You snivelling little creep! Do you know what my housemaster said to me when I begged for mercy, do you?

Bill No, guv. I never went to no public school.

Adrian Really? Well, "Smythe", he'd say, "you should have thought of that before, shouldn't you?" You knew the score when you broke in here, knew what would happen if you were caught, knew what to expect?

Bill Yus, guv, I know but—

Adrian But nothing—now you're trying to wriggle out, playing me for a sentimental fool.

Bill No, guv. I didn't mean—

Adrian It won't get you anywhere, you best know that. I've no time for your sort.

Bill Course you ain't, guv, course you ain't. Wouldn't expect—

Adrian Social pariahs, that's what you are, parasites.

Bill (*hanging his head and walking* DR) Yus, guv, you're right, guv.

Adrian (*replacing the telephone and moving to the upstage end of the settee*) Don't try anything! Of course I'm right. It surprises me that you know it, though.

Bill Mind if I sit down, guv?—feeling a bit shocked.

Adrian Come over all dizzy, have you? Suffer from black-outs, do we? Don't remember forcing an entry, no doubt. Go on. (*Indicating the armchair*) Sit there! I shouldn't bother to try the old "I don't know what come over me" routine, it won't wash with me.

Bill (*sitting and dropping his head in his hands*) Won't try nothin', promise yer that, guv.

Adrian Or, how about the old hard-luck story, the "never had a chance" approach?

Bill You wouldn't be interested in my miserable life, guv, couldn't expect it.

Adrian I'm not and you couldn't—(*sitting on the upstage end of the settee*)—but I'll listen. Make a good after-dinner tale. Go on then, start from where your father used to beat you.

Bill Never had one.

Adrian Oh, better still, and your mother was thrown on to the street to starve. Don't give me that, not in these days of free handouts for scroungers.

Bill Didn't have a bad life as a kid. Me old mum done her best.

Adrian So what led you into a life of crime, then?

Bill Dunno really, hopelessness, I suppose and a little jealousy. See, for blokes like me, it's either sweatin' it out in a factory, just ter get by like, or tryin' ter grab some of what blokes like you have had give yer.

Adrian The old class syndrome, is it, the masses exploited by the privileged few? What a disappointment, and I thought I was going to hear something original. You're out of date, lad, this is the latter half of the twentieth century, the era of equal opportunity.

Bill No, guv, it ain't, that's only what you'd like to believe.

Adrian Nonsense, there's free education: the route to university and the professions is open to anyone with guts and determination. That's the trouble with you lot, spineless. You expect to be wet-nursed, have everything handed to you and if it isn't, you bellyache about unfairness.

Bill I ain't blaming no-one. You see, guv, it's really a question of class attitudes, of conditioning. I ain't ungrateful for what governments have tried to do for the less fortunate—count meself in that group, I do—but that won't put nothing right. What we've gotter do is change how we think: how you thinks of me and how I thinks of you.

Adrian Suddenly very erudite, aren't we?

Bill There you are, see. You thought 'cause I don't speak proper, 'cause I ain't dressed up, that I'm ignorant. Oh, no, guv, I tried them routes you spoke of but it didn't work, did it?

Adrian Don't tell me you've been to university? What were you reading, "Advanced Safebreaking"?

Bill There yer go again, don't yer? Put me in a little box you have: ignorant, stupid, scrounger, villain—all them labels on it, ain't there?

Adrian Well, you hardly express yourself like a graduate, do you? I mean . . .

Bill See, every time you open your mouth, mate, you betray your class prejudice.

Adrian (*rising*) Don't you call me "mate", my man. I'm no mate of yours and besides, I hate the vulgar term.

Bill "Guv" was all right, wan't it? Little bit of the old deference in that, tugging of the old forelock, "God bless the squire" and all that. Absolutely riddled with class prejudice you are, no doubt of that.

Adrian (*standing over him*) Oh, I am, am I? Well if you're an example of the emancipated and enlightened citizen, I'm just glad I am, that's all. (*He moves away from Bill*)

Bill Never said I wan't prejudiced did I? Got all me class attitudes, I have; cause of me downfall.

Adrian (*circling upstage of the settee*) The paragon admits imperfections, does he?

Bill Take deferred gratification.

Adrian (*turning to him*) Deferred what?

Bill Deferred gratification, you know, working for something in the future. I ain't got that, see; stuck with immediate gratification, I am. Can't do something this year which might help me next like, can't wait more than a week for anything.

Adrian (*moving round the settee to* C) Where on earth did you pick up terms like those?

Bill Open University, mate—sorry, guv.

Adrian You joined the Open University?

Bill Not exactly, couldn't afford ter join. Read a few courses in the library, though, and that's what convinced me.

Adrian Convinced you of what?

Bill That I was stuck, fixed, labelled. One of them sociology courses showed me as how I'd got all the classical working-class characteristics.

Adrian Well, that's a help, surely?

Bill What is?

Adrian To know your faults.

Bill I never said nothing about faults. There you go again, see, making class-value judgements.

Adrian If they're not faults, what are they?

Bill Different set of values, no better, no worse. 'Cept that they ain't much help in a society where you blokes make all the rules.

Adrian Me? I don't make any rules.

Bill Not as you're aware of, perhaps, but the whole system's based on your values, guv, well, the values you got from yer parents and yer school. So, naturally, yer think they're right.

Adrian Naturally, and they are.

Bill See what I mean, there yer go again, proving me point.

Adrian (*moving to him*) Just a minute, are you trying to suggest that because you have a different set of "class values", as you call them, that that justifies you breaking into an honest man's house and stealing what he's worked for all his life? Is that what you're saying?

Bill No, all I'm saying is while one group has an advantage over another, there's going ter be a sense of grievance and it's that what leads people in ter crime. If I can't have what he's got legitimately, then I'll get it the other way, see?

Adrian No, I don't. I've never heard so much pseudo-intellectual claptrap in all my life. (*Moving to the telephone*) Right, well, you've had your chance, made your plea—

Bill And it's fallen on deaf ears, eh?

Adrian Not deaf, my man, not deaf; received, understood but rejected. I shouldn't waste any more breath if I were you. Save it for the police. (*Brandishing the poker*) And don't try anything.

The door opens UR *and Helen enters wearing a dressing-gown*

Helen What on earth are you doing down here, Adrian? (*Seeing Bill*) Oh my God, who's he?

Adrian All right, Helen, no need to panic. He won't dare try anything.

Helen But who is he?

Adrian Only a common criminal, a burglar.

Helen Burglar!

Adrian Nothing to worry about.

Helen (*crossing to Adrian's* R) In our house! Nothing to worry about!

Adrian It's all right; he knows who's boss.

Bill Won't give no trouble, missus.

Helen Adrian, he spoke to me!

Adrian Yes, he can speak, rather well, actually. Do you know he's been trying to convince me that his degeneration is all my fault.

Bill Never said that. Trust you ter get the wrong end of the stick.

Helen (*moving to the upstage end of the settee; timorously*) How dare you speak to my husband like that, you beast! (*To Adrian*) Oh dear, what are we going to do?

Adrian I was just about to ring the police. Now you're here, you can do it. That'll make sure he doesn't try anything.

Helen (*taking a step back*) Try anything! He's not violent, is he?

Bill Told him I won't. No good arguing, he don't listen. (*Standing*) Please don't ring them, missus, can't face going down no more.

Helen (*moving to Adrian and taking the telephone from him*) Not ring them? Of course I shall—you deserve all you get, likes of you, breaking into innocent people's houses, stealing . . .

Adrian crosses to the upstage end of the settee and threatens Bill with the poker. Bill sits

Adrian Typical isn't it, absolutely typical? When they're cornered, do they stand up and take it like a man? Oh, no, cringe and wheedle, try to play on our sympathy.

Bill Not thinking of myself. You any idea, missus, what it's like for a man's wife when he's doing time? Left on her own, maybe for years, no money, no respect and her pregnant too.

Adrian Well, well, we've exhausted the rational approach, so now we try the emotional.

Bill Not trying nothing; just dead worried about me missus.

Helen She's no doubt no better than you and deserves all she gets.

Adrian Don't think she really exists, do you? Pregnant wife, my foot! He must think we're green.

Bill Straight up, she don't only exist, she's outside.

Helen Outside?

Adrian The watch-out, of course, knew there'd be one.

Bill Allus work together.

Adrian (*moving round the settee to* DR) How very touching. (*He crosses to Bill, poker raised*) Well, get her in here! Then you can both be together when the police arrive. Come on then, call her from the window and don't try to make a break for it, unless you want a cracked skull!

Bill rises and reluctantly moves up to the french windows as Adrian threatens him with the poker. Adrian follows him

That's far enough! Call her and don't try to warn her or you'll get this!

Bill draws back the curtain a couple of feet, pushes the window open and whistles

Helen (*petrified*) There might be several of them, you can't trust him!

Adrian (*to Helen*) Quick, be ready to dial nine-nine-nine. Pregnant wife, it's pathetic.

Linda appears at the window. She is dressed in jeans, a dirty pullover and looks nine months pregnant

Linda What's up, Bill? (*Seeing Adrian*) Oh, we're copped!

Bill All right, gal, won't hurt yer, come inside.

Linda steps into the room

Adrian Good Lord, she really is.

Helen (*putting down the receiver and crossing to the left of Linda*) The poor thing! (*To Bill*) You great, insensitive brute, you! Fancy making her come out in that state.

Bill Never made her.

Linda No, he never, missus. Wouldn't let him do the job by hisself.

Adrian What loyalty, so touching.

Helen Put that poker down, you stupid man! Can't you see the state the poor girl's in. (*Taking Linda's arm and helping her to the settee*) You come and sit down, dear, you shouldn't be standing around in your state. (*She sits Linda on the downstage end of the settee and then sits beside her*)

Adrian (*to Bill*) Go on, back to your chair!

by kureau

Bill goes and sits in the armchair. Adrian follows him, poker at the ready

Linda You don't need that no more, mister, my Bill wouldn't scarper wivout me.

Adrian (*standing upstage between the chair and the settee*) I'm taking no chances with you two.

Linda Let us go, mister, we'll go straight, honest.

Adrian Oh yes, that's easy to say now, isn't it? I suppose if you'd got away with it, you'd have returned the goods with an apology.

Linda We only done it for the baby.

Bill You wouldn't have lost nothing, insured ain't yer?

Adrian As a matter of fact, no.

Helen They weren't to know that, Adrian. It was for the baby.

Linda Had ter give him a better start than we had.

Bill Would have been our last job.

Linda Couldn't have gone on once he was born. Just enough ter get started, rent a little place, that's all we was after.

Helen Don't you think you should give them the benefit of the doubt, Adrian. After all, we've lost nothing.

Adrian Don't see it; just because she happens to be pregnant, and him—well, not the worst of criminal types I suppose—still, not right, the law's the law. If you break it, you should be punished.

Helen Extenuating circumstances, dear, they have to be considered. (*To Linda*) What you going to call it, dear?

Linda Dunno, hadn't thought, had we, Bill?

Bill Not proper like, no.

Linda If it's a girl, I'd like ter call it after you, missus. You been so kind and everything.

Helen What a nice thought, dear. We've never had any children. That would be very nice.

Linda Don't know yer name, though.

Helen Oh, it's Helen, dear, Helen. So what would it be, Helen what?

Linda Smith.

Helen Helen Smith, well that's not so very different from my name is it—Smythe?

Linda No, funny ain't it?

Helen Helen Smythe, Helen Smith.

Bill What if it's a boy, Lin?

Linda Call him Adrian, then, shall we? (*To Helen*) That's right, ain't it? Your husband?

Adrian Very touching. Now, I suppose I should be so flattered that I let bygones be bygones.

Helen Perhaps this once, Adrian, we might forget principles, eh? After all, humanity's more important.

Adrian Humanity or stupidity?

Bill You won't regret it, mate—squire.

Adrian Squire is it now? The final touch of flattery.

Linda (*sobbing*) Please Mr Smythe, please, give us one more chance.

Bill You ain't lost nothing, squire—mister.

Linda Little home for our baby, all we wanted. You've got everything, give us a chance.

Adrian Oh, yes, we've got everything haven't we? The privileged we are, the exploiters of the under-dog. Well, let me tell you something, Mrs Smith—it is Mrs, is it?

Bill Will be soon as—

Linda Soon as we got somewhere ter live.

Adrian Well, let me tell you, you're much better off than we are.

Bill Come on, mate, don't try that one on us: the "burden of the rich man" yarn. We got eyes—little car in the garage out there.

Adrian Ah, so you were going to take that as well were you?

Bill Not my line, mate. Noticed it though when I cased yer.

Helen Cased?

Adrian He means sizing the job up, dear, like giving an estimate.

Linda Cosy house, lovely furniture, we couldn't never be as grand as you.

Adrian (*moving behind the settee*) No, well perhaps you won't want to be when I tell you we have less than nothing. (*Leaning over Linda's shoulder*) Like the furniture do you? Good, I'll like it better when it's paid for. Know what that costs me a month? Twenty quid. (*He moves round to Bill*) Then that little car you mentioned, that's not mine either—fifty quid a month. Then there's the mortgage, a mere seventy quid. (*He goes to the bookcase*) To say nothing of insurances, Barclaycard, Access, rates and God knows what. (*Turning to them*) Hundreds in debt, I am. If I work till I'm seventy, I can't pay it all off. And that's the real difference between us: you're free and I'm condemned to slave at a desk, nine till five, just to keep myself out of bankruptcy. (*He moves to the bureau chair*) I'm sentenced to life doing a job I hate so why should I let you get off from a miserly ten years, answer me that?

Bill gets up and, going over to Adrian, puts his hand on Adrian's shoulder

Bill Hell, lummy mate, didn't realize. Is that what going straight means? Thought you blokes had it easy, I did.

Helen There, you see, we never know about other people. To think I was ready to turn you in. You're not a bit like I thought. Just fancy, Helen Smith.

Linda Well, we're not having any of those credit card things when we're wed, Bill Smith, that's for sure.

Bill Hundreds in debt, you say?

Adrian Thousands probably, if I add it all up.

Bill And you wan't insured?

Adrian Couldn't afford it could we?—got enough millstones.

Linda And we don't owe a penny, well I never.

Helen Goes to show, Linda, we should never envy others. You don't mind if I call you Linda, dear?

Linda Course not—Helen.

Helen That's nice.

Adrian (*putting down the poker beside the bureau*) Sorry about this, er—Bill, old man, wouldn't have used it you know, just bluffing.

Bill That's all right, guv—Adrian, me old lad, knew yer wouldn't. Could see you wan't the type. (*He reaches under his coat and takes out the bag of ornaments*) Look, hope yer don't take this wrong but here's what I nicked before you nabbed me. Didn't know you wan't insured, did I? (*He puts the bag beside the bureau*)

Adrian (*sitting*) Very decent of you, Bill, old man. Just shows how wrong one can be about people doesn't it?

Bill It's the labels what does it, Adrian, old son.

Linda (*to Adrian*) You ain't a-going to turn us in now, are yer?

Helen Turn you in, dear? He'll have me to reckon with if he does.

Adrian Turn you in? Course I'm not. I shall count tonight as an experience, a broadening of my understanding of the world.

(*Rising*) Tell you what, it's a bit premature, but let's have a little drink to the future.

Linda I dunno, yer supposed ter wait till it's born. Might mean a bit a bad luck.

Adrian Nonsense, you're not superstitious are you, Bill?

Bill Never like ter drink when I'm working.

Adrian But you're not working now, I hope.

Bill No, that's right enough.

Helen Well, it can just be to celebrate our meeting.

Adrian Our new understanding. (*He moves towards the armchair*) What do you say, Linda?

Linda What you think, Bill?

Bill (*moving to the upstage end of the settee*) Don't see no harm.

Adrian Good, that's settled then. Now what shall we have?

Bill What yer got?

Adrian No beer, I'm afraid, whisky, brandy, sherry, gin.

Helen I don't think she should have gin, dear. She really shouldn't have alcohol.

Adrian Hear that, Linda, doctor says no alcohol? How about a bitter lemon, would that suit?

Linda That'll do nice. Anything really.

Adrian You, Bill?

Bill Wouldn't mind a whisky, not a big'un.

Adrian Right, one whisky, one bitter lemon and what shall we have, Helen, sherry?

Helen I don't mind, dear, not used to drinking in the early hours. Perhaps a coffee would be—

Adrian Can't celebrate with a coffee, woman. (*Pulling Helen to her feet*) Come on, we'll get the drinks.

Adrian starts to guide Helen towards the door

Linda You ain't afraid we'll scarper then?

Adrian (*turning to her*) Scarper? What on earth is there to scarper from?

Helen We're not at all worried, dear, are we, Adrian? We trust you both.

Adrian Absolutely. (*He gets the bag of ornaments and gives it to Bill*) Tell you what, old man, you arrange these round the room for me, never can remember where they go. (*To Helen*) Come on, old girl, or it'll be time for breakfast.

Adrian and Helen exit

Bill (*moving to the coffee table*) Well, gal, would you credit it?

Linda Don't like it, Bill, do you? Reckon we ought ter nip off?

Bill stares at the bag of ornaments. There is a pause

(*Rising*) Well, do yer?

Bill (*coming to a sudden conclusion*) No, gal, I don't. Go on, sit down!

Linda (*sitting*) What then?

Bill I'm going ter put this lot back where I found 'em.

During the following dialogue, he moves round the room replacing the ornaments, starting with the bureau and then moving to the bookcase

Linda Blimey!

Bill I ain't gone barmy, gal. All of a sudden, I feel like I was someone. Nobody ain't never said they trusted me afore and I like the feel on it. Blokes like him don't usually even speak ter the likes of me, just sticks their noses in the air like I was a bad smell or something. Well, Adrian ain't like that and maybe lots of 'em ain't bad blokes when yer gets ter know 'em. I'd labelled him like what he had me. Well, it's a real eye-opener.

Linda Yeah, fancy him owing all that lolly.

Bill We allus reckons them what's different from us has a better time of it. We gets jealous, starts to hate 'em and blame 'em for all our troubles. Well, I'm going to show him that we're just like him; honest to them what's honest to us.

Linda Bill, we ain't going ter let on everything, are we?

Bill (*moving to Linda*) Everything, gal. We'll let 'em see just how much we trust 'em.

Linda They won't like it. Might not understand.

Bill Gotter take that risk, gal. It's gotter be a new beginning for us, a fresh start. We gotter come clean about everything.

Linda But what'll she think?

Bill Everything, gal, no buts.

Linda (*rising*) If you say so, Bill. Hope yer know what yer doing. (*She turns from the audience and extracts a large cushion from her jeans and then holds it up*) What'll I do with this?

Bill Put it behind yer, we'll have a good laugh.

Linda (*placing the cushion behind her and sitting on the settee*)
You hope.

Bill (*going and sitting in the armchair*) No, they'll understand
when we tell 'em.

Adrian enters with a tray of drinks, followed by Helen

Adrian (*placing the drinks on the coffee table*) Here we are then,
sorry we took so long.

Helen (*sitting on the settee beside Linda*) Had to wash the glasses.
Haven't been used for ages.

Adrian (*handing round the drinks*) Whisky for you, Bill. Sorry,
Linda, should have been ladies first. Here you are, bitter lemon.
Sherry for Helen and one for me. (*He stands* DR) Now here's
to new understanding.

They all drink

Hey, don't down it all, we have another toast. Here's to the
future young Smith and . . . (*He breaks off, staring at Linda*)
Good grief!

Helen (*following his gaze*) What? I don't believe . . .

Linda (*standing up*) It's all right, ain't had a miscarriage. (*Holding
up the cushion*) All it was.

Helen (*rising quickly*) You mean you weren't? You little bitch!
How could you! (*Glaring at Linda, she deliberately places her
glass on the table and then, suddenly, darts up and picks up the
poker from the side of the bureau and runs round the back of the
sofa to thrust it into Adrian's hand*) Take that and if either of
them move, hit them! (*She rushes to the telephone*)

Adrian, with his eyes on Bill, backs UL *and places his drink on the
bureau*

Bill (*rising*) Look, I can explain.

Adrian (*crossing quickly* UR *to above settee*) Sit down or you'll
get it.

Bill sits

Linda (*rising*) You don't understand.

Helen (*picking up the receiver*) I understand only too well.

Adrian Hold it a minute, Helen.

Helen Why should I?

Linda Know it's a bit of a shock but . . .

Adrian Look, Bill's replaced all the ornaments, that shows something.

Bill Had ter come clean on everything. Couldn't cheat yer, yer see.

Linda It's an old trick ter dodge the cops.

Adrian Trick?

Linda Excuse ter be out in the middle of the night: he's getting me ter hospital, see.

Bill Cop car took us once.

Linda Near old go that was.

Bill Nipped out while they was fetching a doctor.

Helen (*replacing the receiver and moving over to Adrian*) So you didn't set out to deceive us then, just the police?

Bill That's right.

Adrian You see, Helen. Don't you think we should be magnanimous and forgive?

Helen Well I—it was a terrible shock.

Bill We're sorry, ain't we Linda?

Linda Yeah.

Helen (*to Adrian*) Put down that ridiculous poker. (*She returns to her seat*) I think I need to sit down.

Adrian places the poker beside the armchair and draws the bureau chair forward so as to sit near Bill

Adrian (*sitting*) Good job you didn't try anything. Couldn't have used it you know, Bill.

Bill I know that, mate.

Linda Sorry, Helen.

Helen No, I'm sorry. I wasn't going to ring them, you know. I was just hurt, that's all.

Linda It's all right, wouldn't have blamed yer.

Adrian Funny when you think about it.

Bill Said you wanted a good after-dinner story.

Adrian Better than I ever imagined.

Linda (*to Helen*) When I do have one, I'll call it Helen.

Bill Or Adrian.

Linda Or Adrian, yes.

Bill (*rising*) Well, suppose we better scarper. Let you get a bit of shut-eye. Could use a bit myself.

Adrian gets up and replaces the bureau chair

Helen Must be awful, always on nights.

Bill Not any more, though, eh Linda?

Linda Done our last job, that's for sure. Next time I have a bump, it'll be for real.

Bill (*holding his hand out to Adrian*) Well, thanks, Adrian, you made a new man out of me, I can tell yer.

Linda (*standing*) Bye, Helen, won't forget about the baby.

Adrian (*moving to Bill and shaking his hand*) Been quite an education, old man.

Helen Mustn't lose touch, must we?

There is the sound of a car drawing up outside

Adrian Good God, who the devil!

Bill (*cringing back* DL) Not the cops!

Linda (*shrinking back* DR) No, Bill, no!

Helen Can't be. Go and see, Adrian, quick!

Adrian rushes up to the window and peers out

Adrian Great Scott, it's the Watson-Smythes!

Helen (*rushing up to the window*) Can't be, they're in Spain!

Adrian It is, I tell you!

Bill Watson-Smythes, who the hell are they?

Adrian Only the owners, you stupid clod!

Bill Owners? You're the owners!

Helen Don't make me laugh.

Linda What's he mean, Bill, owners?

Bill (*picking up the poker and advancing on Adrian*) You stinking, lying, little—

Adrian No need for that, Bill, old man.

Linda darts R *to bar the door*

Bill You pair of twisting cons! So all that crap about mortgages and that was all ruddy lies!

Adrian dodges DR *and Bill faces him over the settee*

Adrian Now, Bill, you don't understand.

As Bill circles left round the downstage end of the settee Adrian moves to the upstage end

Bill I understand all right, you middle-class bastard!

Adrian Please, Bill, they're the bastards, the Watson-Smythes: your real enemies, yours and mine. They've got us both trapped, don't you understand? They own everything, control everything.

There is the sound of car doors being slammed

Helen (*moving to Adrian's right side*) They'll be here in a minute! Please, Bill! Linda!

Bil (*to Linda*) Grab her, gal, she's no better than him!

Linda moves over and grasps Helen's right wrist

Helen Let go, you little bitch! I'll—

Linda Scratch yer eyes out, you try anything!

Adrian Bill, please, they'll get us all!

Bill Let them. See who they thinks is the real villains.

Helen That lot don't care: justice for them is coming out on top.

Adrian She's right, Bill, they'll do for the lot of us.

Bill Let them, as long as they gets you two.

Linda (*letting go of Helen and staggering*) Bill, Bill, I feel funny! I—everything's going . . . (*She collapses on the settee*)

Bill (*staggering*) What the . . .? Here, what the hell? (*He staggers DL and collapses across the armchair*)

Adrian (*to Helen*) Quick, upstairs! We can sneak out later. (*He propels her to the door*)

Helen What's happened? I don't understand.

Adrian A little precaution, dear, you can't trust their sort.

Helen Something in their drink?

Adrian Harmless, but they'll be out long enough. Come on! They'll get the police up as soon as they find them.

Helen What about the car?

Adrian They can have the credit for that. We'll soon get another.

Helen exits

(*Holding the door handle, ready to close it; looking back into the room*) So long, suckers. You've got a lot to learn yet about surviving, poor, naïve bastards.

Adrian exits and closes the door softly behind him

Footsteps are heard approaching off as—

                                    the CURTAIN *falls*

FURNITURE AND PROPERTY LIST

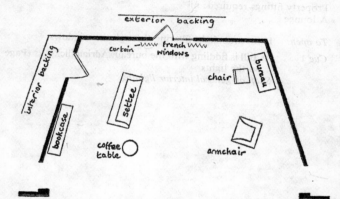

On stage: Bookcase. *On it:* a number of ornaments
Small settee
Coffee table
Armchair
Bureau. *On it:* various ornaments, telephone
Bureau chair
Window curtains, open to start

Off stage: Torch **(Bill)**
Poker **(Adrian)**
Tray. *On it:* glass of whisky, 2 sherries, bitter lemon
(Adrian)

Personal: **Bill:** bag for ornaments attached to jacket lining, lock-
picking instrument in pocket
Linda: cushion, for padding

LIGHTING PLOT

Property fittings required: nil
A lounge

To open: Faint moonlight filtering through the windows

Cue 1   As **Bill** is fiddling with the bureau, **Adrian** flicks   (Page 1)
           on the lights
           Snap on general interior lighting

EFFECTS PLOT

MADE AND PRINTED IN GREAT BRITAIN BY
LATIMER TREND & COMPANY LTD PLYMOUTH
MADE IN ENGLAND